When All You Are Is Change

Ambica Gossain

For the One
who left me behind
(to find meaning
in the rest of my life)

To the Instagram poetry community -
for ushering words beneath my metaphorical wings.
For instilling in me the faith that my
words hold the weight of hope, guiding others as
they navigate this ever-changing journey of life.
Your support, resonance, and shared vulnerability remind
me that poetry is not just written.
It is felt, lived and set free.

TABLE OF CONTENTS

A parabola (n) is the trajectory of an object in free fall under uniform gravity, neglecting air resistance. Its path curves symmetrically, with a highest point (vertex) where upward motion transitions to downward motion.

*Halliday, David, Resnick, Robert & Walker, Jearl
Fundamentals of Physics, Wiley 9

PATH OF PERSISTENCE

A BREACH

What is balance?
If not overflow despite
a breach in a dam.
What is balance?
But a float to the surface-
gasp-of-truth refusal
to swallow (about) yourself.

Love is not a river
that flows despite.
It flows in spite of
the only obstruction
that blocks it.
You.

PLACENTA

Choices
already made.
Cells dividing
to form
the bulk of me.
Floating in the
life-water dark
of an amniotic sac.

EXILED

My feet touch back down
on uneven ground studded
with mounds of cow dung.
An unofficial welcome fashioned
into a dangerous obstacle course.

Spiced winds hand-whisked
in rambunctious kitchens
tickle my nostrils.
Before dosing me with the
stench of sewage from their backyards.

The turbine engines that
brought me back still running,
making my head want to bolt.
But my heart feels this home,
deep down in my conflicted bones.
I cannot deny that beauty
is indeed only skin deep.

BLUE

I am the blue of a daughter
(left wanting.)
An unopened gift collecting dust
from a parent's absence.
I am the portrait of a haunting,
seduced by the faintest allusion
to a father figure
(validation in all the wrong arms.)
What better way
to navigate history and
not be swallowed myself?
I stall the clock of the past
just long enough to catch up.

ANYWAY

All my skin
can't contain
the sins within

So when I say
you're my true north,
the list of things
I'm not sorry for

Or I can't decide which is worse
losing you or letting you stay
I know I'm doomed either way.

What I really mean
is I love you (anyway)

DIRTY DISHES

Fog rolls in.
The dirty dishes
pile higher in the sink.

The therapist asks
do I believe in life
after love?
It's more punishing
to remember than to forget
the years I spent worshipping a drought.

EPI-LOG

If our expression of love
is first forged by the brush
of a mother's tender bosom,
then its nuances shelter
in a father's origami arms.
Its living script eventually
nipped and tucked at the intersection
of nature and nurture.
An ever evolving duality of who
we are
and where we've been.

MESSY

Yearning for more
settling for less
I pull the trigger

Words
blow-out
my brains instead
I let poetry
clean up the mess

HATCHET HANDS

Daggers drawn bleed love (mine).
Who am I kidding
with a white flag heart
and hatchet hands?
Peace is a vanishing point
with my fight cut down to size
and a burial that binds.
So be it.

NOOSE

I threw you a lifeline
and you noosed it
to strangle me

DEAR BODY

My dear, dear body
Mon cher torse.
I have used you, abused you,
Paid penance by blood
for every morsel of affection
you ever dared to consume.
Fractured the bones
of my permanent home to
make femur fantasies come true.

I've conceived and I've carried
(validation) to term.
To prove life worthy
to be in my womb.

Pricked your veins with oxytocin
to induce the contractions.
Deliver baby-good news
along with my real issues;

the curvaceous playing field
of my dominant demons.
In exchange for your submissive
shades of black and blue.

As if that were not enough
thrust you into headlights
to fight for your life when
you asked me what to do.

My dear devoured body
you've patiently persisted
in standing by me.
Now it's time
I finally stand by you.

ROADS TO SOMEWHERE

SWALLOW

I am many people
My amorphous identity defended
by a multi-headed Hindu God
Relinquished to the speculative distance
between your censorious interpretations
and my own mythical representation

Each face
designed to indulge
a particular palate
I am a potent cocktail
of stirred spirit selves
Sparking the heady rush
you need to swallow me

LOST

He told me to hold my tongue
And that's how I lost my voice
He told me to turn a blind eye
And that's how I lost my sight
He told me to turn a deaf ear
And that's how I lost my hearing
He told me to hold my breath
And that's how I lost my sense of smell
He told me to put it on ice
And that's how I lost my soul
He told me to start a fire
And just like that
The story ended

I MISS MYSELF

I miss myself,
the narration of me
The who I would be
if I didn't choose
the me I am now

I miss myself
so damn much
I have no
bandwidth
to miss you too

FINAL RESTING PLACE?

Chaise lounge
and a cocktail.
Whiskey-wet safety
stings my lips.

I am sick
of living in reaction.
Bound by the
leftovers from others
that I am force-fed
until I grow numb.

I die a little more
each time I cut myself
down to size, minimize.
To fit neatly inside
the others' clenched- fist need
to be heard over me.

Still alive.

BLANK SLATE

Things you only write about when
you're in the heart of them or (they)

are in the mouth of you
The day my name stopped tasting fearless

Like the tug at my teeth when airborne and
a mountain climber's roped delight of poetry

unspools down a deathly drop
A silky web of reserve dental floss

across my jaw's rocky range
A hit or miss watching its step

between cavernous budding cavities
and chipped-toothed sharkness

As if it were enough to prevent gravity
from claiming them

Maybe that's what I imagine
a smile you can't trust looks like

Grief scruffing it toothless
My lips stop kissing confidence

full on the mouth when a futility of surplus
mint paste squirts from too huge an orifice

The oldest trick in the book invented to con you
into buying more of what you don't need
(my own poetry included)

There has to be a reason I dream
words toppling off the toothbrush

and dancing into darkness
of a scrunch red face

from the sour taste a tongue can't rid itself of
And its corresponding sick in the stomach

from more tomato ketchup than fattening chips
If the cholesterol doesn't kill you

preservatives most certainly will
plummet you to a cancerous demise

How many poems need to read ridiculous
for me to be rendered immortal?

CHIPS

Finally alone
with my favorite
companion.
Spicy yes?
Salty?
She can be.
A sensory overload
A dance on hot coals.
Another day of gratitude
for living among truths.
That ulcer.
The remedial chug
of a chaser.
Beer for a belly of distraction.
Diet coke for an aspartame
fizz of forgetting things.
That sting to be remembered.

WELL FED

You can search
my closet for skeletons.
But I feed them too well
to ever be found.
I don't know who I am
without the bones I'd rather forget.

HUNGOVER

Hungover. (Again.)
Throwing em' back
is as good as the truth
that slurs in its stead.
Unresolved mixes my drinks,
throbs me a headache
of not stirred.
A landmine of the unexpressed
shaken to explode.
I float to the WC only to vomit what
I never developed a stomach for.
Self preservation
is the fragmented indigestion
of burning a hole in memory.
Amnesia is the lonely stagger
from my head to my heart.
Home?

BODY & MIND

It's a shame
to feel all the world's pain.
My body and mind opponents
of a writer's purpose.
That just won't be.
Shit.
And still I feel the empty
(of a blank page.)

TOUCHED

I had nothing to give you
(I was someone else's to love)
And yet my selfish heart wanted you
To offer me the moon.
And everything its light touched
Just so I could turn it away.

THE BOTTOM LINE

It wouldn't have mattered
that you didn't love me as much.
If I had just loved myself
enough for the both of us.

A MATCHLESS FLAME

KEEPING TIME

Time can be ribbon
Or metal links of pain
A keeping of a static
When all you are is change

CONVEX OR CONCAVE?

We were both lusting,
you for me.
And I, for the wonder.
There was never a point
where we'd converge.

SPEAK WITHIN THE SILENCE

My words, a thread I bead with rhyme and
string together mellifluously with rhythm
Ring insincere
adorned with superfluous embellishments
Their essence stripped,
entombed in an ornamental casket
They shimmer like a bejeweled
treasure chest of empty promises
But I fear without them,
you may not accept them nor find them attractive
Thus rejecting me
So perhaps they're best left
six feet under this false pretense
This mud I cake my face with everyday to belong
Perhaps that's the only way to keep them alive;
to speak within this silence

INTENTIONAL FORGETFULNESS

To wake
and (not) remember
the damage done
Is hating yourself
if you do

A DIFFERENT NAME

I found love
for you in the
despicable place
Where I stow hate
and conceal shame
Demanding I give it
a different name

DESERTED

I've always regretted
not growing to love flowers.
Chalk it up to my first introduction:
bulbs planted in a desert womb.
That needed an extra push for roots to catch life.
But my mother's tears were otherwise engaged
watering a greener garden inside her head.
I got used to seeing dead tulips
where poetry bloomed in red.

TWILIGHT TIPTOES

Twilight tiptoes troubled times
Its stealthy shadows casting fear's
net over a cradled child
Armed with candles and crosses
a mother endeavors to ward off
the confounding disquiet
Horns locked with her circadian rhythm
sleep knocks a jackhammer pulse
from the devil's side
White knuckled resilience needing to preside
over words from the heart's helpline to
keep her open-eyed

THIS & THAT

I was a
lot of
things.
I was
this. I
was that.
And now
that I'm
not where
am I at?

PERMISSION

Your heart doesn't ask your permission
before falling hopelessly for the thing you can't have.
Then splintering into pieces that can never be part
of anything whole again.

WINTER SOLSTICE

In a world where I had everything
I wanted you (to stick out like a sore thumb)
Red flag raised, salt-like praise
On feverish skin, my own winter solstice
Flooding my privileged life with darkness
More myself than I was

I AM MY OWN REFUGE

I know you feel
like we have nothing in common.
That the language
I speak is foreign.

But don't you ask yourself why
your tears seek my refuge to dry?
Why your frantic heart slows
in the shade of my boughs?
Why your restless soul roots
in my burgeoning shoots?

Why your weary feet answer
my summoning susurrations?
Don't you recognize
those whispers as your own?

A HIGHER POWER

A COOK'S PRAYER

So what should I make
of his red-eyed glare?
Hurtling daggers at me
with samurai precision.
I churn his contempt
in the grind of my mixer.
Whisk his anger with some chill
(to ice it down a notch.)
I breathe in the only thing I can:
the distance I must traverse
for the hate to leave this man.

HAGGLE

For the price of my soul
You are everything I want
If I told you this truth
Would you continue
To be my lie?

SANCTUARY

I pushed them down
and buried them deep:
my woes under the ground
for the earth to keep.
But when I opened my eyes,
they were staring back at me,
my furrowed brow their sanctuary.

PEACE ON EARTH

Let it fall away. Let it crumble.
The mountain of expectation
casting its foreboding shadow.
Where sunny intentions
should frolic carefree.
Vulnerability tethered only
to our morality.
Let gratitude come from
brazen benevolence,
the unconditional giving of one's soul.
Let me not ask you what you can do for me,
but ask myself what I can do for you instead.
My actions gratuitous, independent
of your calculated reaction
as I circumvent tricks
of light and animation.
To shoot love from the sterling center of
my unalloyed heart.
The hearth and home
of peace on earth within you.

GOD

His voice answered
unsolicited prayers my heart
didn't even know to invoke.

SHAPE AND SIZE

Verbalized
Hopelessness billows
the shape and size
Of my identity.

LIGHT

Perhaps the most beautiful thing
about the darkness is its inability
to be broken by anything
other than the piercing rays of the sun.

LOYALTY

I'll be a pawn,
the front-liner pride
of your collateral damage.
Slugs lodged
where loyalty resides.

HEAVY

Take my heavy chain
and link it to a dead weight,
I can't carry it another day.
Let it sink to the bottom of the ocean,
and deep dive my pain away.
I've forgotten how to breathe.

APPLE WATCH

I've laid claim to my dead father's watch.
Apple.
It pulsates a warmth on my wrist
the way it must have hugged his.
Records my heart skip multiple beats
when it last recorded his heart.
Stopping.

It transports me back in time.
Dorothy, flailing in a tornado of
coffee, cologne and cigarettes.
En route to the paternal Wizard of Oz
"If wishes were horses, beggars would ride," my
wristwatch warned.

Still I'd spend four decades
face down, tethered to one's tail.
Determined to mount a stud for
no one's taking or everyone's?
If an illusion is to be believed.

The rope snaps.
The sudden of his wake up alarm.
Six-thirty.
Instinct reaches to dial his
syrupy thick coat of morning throat.

Little schoolgirl shoes flying off
moments after mother painstakingly dressed me.
My pigtails cascading truant.
A uniform wrinkled from climbing back
into bed, my entirety curled into the nook
of a chest carved in the shape of me.

My son's present nose
burrows deep into my fabric.
And for once I don't resist and pull away.
Letting him indent the only kind of memory
a heart imprints.
After everything else is long gone.

CRAVE BEAUTIFUL ENDINGS

I don't care for journeys.
I crave beautiful endings.
Doesn't matter what you said
when I was alive,
but what you'll do when I am gone.
Reminisce how I gave it all,
so the life we chose didn't
become the trap we didn't.
I don't want you to break down,
drown yourself in tears.
Let the adoration I felt
linger in everything I touched.
Make the dreams I contrived
as important as the ones I sacrificed.
So my soul means more than my body ever did.
I ask to be remembered with deep affection
and not forgotten with regret.
Grant me this, my love, and I shall fade
gracefully into the night.

QUESTIONS TO REVELATION

ON REPEAT

I start a poem
with "I" again
Self indulgence opens my day.
A habit of mine even if it's
simply words that rhyme.
Pause or 'play me' time?
Will guilt fast forward me
to another blank page today?

OF COURSE

Of course. I care.
Love is semantics.
Nouns and verbs.
I never learned.
At the end of the day
It's just a bridging of
our distance.
What speaks from my heart
and what you never hear,
waiting for the words instead.

MOSQUITO

Dusk drones a tug of war with the tropics
on my picket fenced porch.
Lizards. With their trigger ready tongues.
A flop wing reconnaissance of low flying bats
nosedive into a swarm of clueless mosquitos.
The clammy threat of those imminent stings
Webbing me in their food chain – averted.

My eyes dart purposefully
between the front door and the usual spot
soon to be occupied by my husband.
I camouflage in the descending shadows,
insect repellent fading fast
but still slower than the minutes before
I am summoned back inside.

The lizards scatter,
defeated by the droppings of the greedy bats.
They hurry back under the porch
to the shaded rocks that protect them.
A harbinger reflex whips my head
in the direction of the crunch underfoot.
Hitching my breath to a halt.

Expectant eyes (mine) part
the heat wave like Moses,
collude with those of the young man
from the wrong side of town,
who makes an accomplice of me,
by cycling past everyday
at that precise moment.
Hunger, a different sting we exchange.
Stung.

Unsuspecting moths to each
Other's ruinous flame,
we burn the long wick of the short lane.
A silent crackle by embers of
words never exchanged.
To stoke a poem that is ours alone.
A magnetic want putting the heavy
wet of the early evening to shame.
Drenched.

I hear my name shouted in abrupt chorus and
return an over my shoulder "coming" into the air.
Air conditioning has a way
of catching up with stolen moments.
I am grateful for the goosebumps.

CONQUER THE WORLD

My father
Always rose in the air
Above his world of chaos
Dodging bullets and bouquets
His warrior lesson
Meant to course my veins
With love and cracked lightning

HEARTBREAKER

Darling, breathe
I was only meant to be
a surge on your EKG

Faltering and flatlining
into the epiphany
that heartbreak is the
first brick in the foundation
of your happily ever after

FALLING

I am in love
with falling in love.
The simultaneous running
into it and out of it.
My heart's predictable pace
in a knee jerk jog on a
gritty earth treadmill of uncertainty.

The spring in my step on the rubberized track
(soft yet sturdy to minimize injury.)
The fall in love that makes
a trail of airborne dust tracing a
journey back to the longer memory
of arms known best, only to take off again.

I revel in the adrenaline filled uneven breaths.
The infinite possibility when you skydive
from a plane just before you open the
parachute to counter gravity with resistance.
Senses tantalized by a whirlwind of desire,
limbs feeling for their bearings.
A heart dangling dangerously close to
its supposed demise.
The going-for-it, death defying,
panoramic view for just a moment of
a "Camelot" life.

SKIN

I searched for a higher purpose.
I made the naïve presumption that
I was made for more.
But what if my only Karma was
to accept the skin my soul wore?

ALIBIS

It's become too easy
to believe what I write is real.
I always cry words
no matter what I feel.
I do it to survive.
I do it to conceal.
Create airtight alibis
so no one sees me cry
real tears.

WINDOW

You need for me
to stay the same
When my heart desires
me to change.
If tomorrow comes without me
know the window of my wanton soul
Opened the blinds
to the fateful light of day

PERISHABLE THOUGHTS

Memories
Sentenced to oblivion
Never created?
Or simply erased.
Either irretrievable.
My "truth" withheld.

THE BIG BANG

In the end we are all made
of the same heavenly stardust.
Irrespective of cast, creed and race,
this naked truth we can trust.
Strip away the extraneous vestments
and embellishments to reveal,
Our skin, bones and celestial flesh
have nothing remarkable to conceal
But the amalgamated remains of the
cosmic collisions of dust, moons and stars.
With the only difference being
the bodily placement of crevices and scars.

VOLUME OF SELF

TALL ORDER

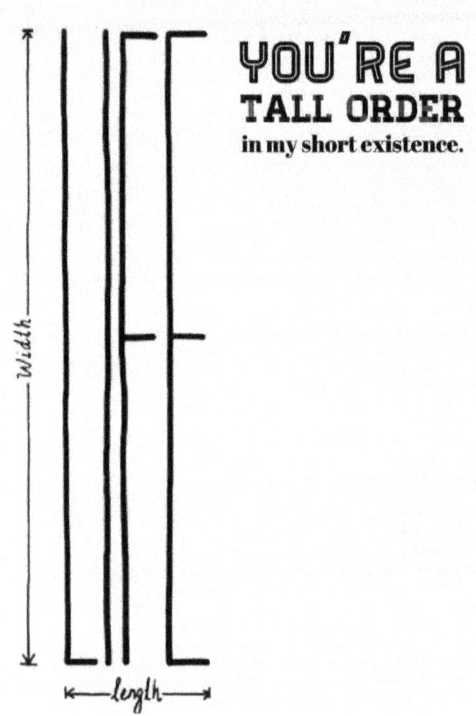

A MOTHER'S HOPE

Hope lives in the way a mother invokes
her son's name like a prayer
In the decisive seconds
before he turns his head to answer
His little boy missing-a-tooth smile
flashed over his shoulder
In her catching his eye and
holding his gaze like asphalt does the heat

In giving him simple instructions
and getting him to repeat
In the handful of lucid words
that escape the maze his babble weaves
In him placing his trust in another human being
In doing away with his training wheels

A mother's hope for her son takes faltering
steps forward and as small as his feet
And sometimes equal steps back
when stumped by what cannot be

As long as each one lands in
the direction of his independence
She'll keep conjuring his name
with each bead of her rosary
Until death visits her mortality

DUMB CHARADES

In time trust can
became an unusual name
For a twisted game.
where you commit a crime
then I take the blame
And no one wins

WHAT LOVE ISN'T?

Write me a love
that doesn't deliberate madness
with trigger-happy fingers
wrapped around expendable lives

Text me a love
that won't steal the sanctity of silence
with a song bereft of words
in the name of a bogus peace

Type me a love
that doesn't bloom in hymns for the lost
And wither in moonlight serenades.
that won't gouge the gifts of a sunrise
Into citrus wounds of a miserable sunset

And if it spins a cycle
of mutually assured destruction
that fails to remove the 'stains'
please write me a love
that doesn't rinse and repeat

NATURE MAGNIFIED

I am my mother's silence
and perhaps my father's s (sometimes) indiscretion
More than just my parent's genes
I've grown a will of titanium
And a wall fortified by a bastion
of bone marrow strength
Not even a hint of injustice
dares to breach

LET'S

Let's not do this
Talk about the things
that could go wrong
Because they will
if they must
and life is too short
For me to chase
and too hard for me to face

Let's live an illusion of happiness
and believe it to be truth
So that the stars are forced
to realign themselves with our vision
The way the world should be

Let's do this
Imagine every minute detail
of our Utopia and make it
A reality with
the conviction of our hearts

If for no other reason
simply because it is a better
way to live
And the easier way
to breathe

HOPE CONCEIVED

Unlike the
cosmos with
Energy
Neither created
nor destroyed
It takes
only belief
For hope
to be conceived
From a void

PILLOW TALK

Lust is an
escape room
filled with
parental failings
And a hundred regrets

A single
filament lightbulb
swings overhead
That you hope
doesn't go out
Before the wishbone
at the cusp of your thighs
Snaps back into place
and your prayers
Go unanswered

WORSHIP

Worship me like
a condemned sailor
Steering into a storm
With savage vehemence
that fossils me
Into your bones

LIFE LEFT

Life. Left. His body.
Then the stories surrounding
him were given free poetic license
To enter the morgue unfiltered or fact checked
(loose lips and big mouths)

Perhaps they had high hopes
of hastening the leave of his spirit
His masculine swirl of energy
still looming overhead the hospital bed
Unsure of its final exit; a respite of heaven
or dance and dodge from the flames of hell

Or were they warding off
the threat of a come back?
His ghoulish haunting of
countless narrators and detractors
And their unfinished business

His death began the unraveling
of a father's 'charitable heart'
My identity once morphed by a
version of him I thought I knew
Now challenged, brought into question
by everything I hadn't known at all

Who are we then, who am I?
If not a combination of all our own pieces
Mixed with the ones of the others
that live inside us (metaphorically)
And when those pieces are suddenly
switched out for ones we don't recognize at all
we are left with a journey of stripping down bare
just to make ourselves whole again

THE QUIETUDE

Caught
in a crossfire of synapses
Starving
to signal the electricity
of creativity
I found the quietude
to flint my own spark
Erupt my own flames
Give my heart back
to the only person who matters
If I am truly
to love another
Myself

ABOUT THE POET

Ambica is a writer, poet and an all-around celebrant of life's unexpected moments. She graduated from *Oberlin College*, USA, with a Bachelor's degree in Biochemistry. To her surprise, also earning her the distinction of Phi Beta Kappa.

Ambica's early curiosity and spark for adventure created her innate drive for what's next - and a never one to stick to a single lane fearlessness. As a result she's happily worn many hats; as a French and English instructor for professionals, an entrepreneur in her family's security system manufacturing business, a guest columnist for the *Hindustan Times* and more.

Her decade long journey as a poet began in the least glamorous way possible—through sheer sleep deprivation after the birth of her second child. What started as an effort to stay awake during diaper changes morphed into an all-consuming passion. Resulting in a collection of over a thousand original poems and ultimately inspiring Ambica to found @heartofquill, a poetry platform dedicated to uplifting diverse poetic voices, at the start of the COVID pandemic.

More recently Ambica's creative passions led to an expansion into hosting soft skills, creative writing, and business English workshops for kids, believing adults aren't the only ones allowed to have fun with words.

Ambica's works explore the beauty and chaos of the human experience, weaving together themes of love, loss, healing, and the quiet art of surviving one's own thoughts. She is a two-time winner of the *People's Choice Award by A.B. Baird Publishing*. Her poetry has been featured in multiple publications including *Baird's* poetry anthology *Like Frost on the Winter Garden, Arboreal Magazine, Gypsophilazine Magazine, t'Art Press, 100 Subtexts Magazine, Querencia Press, Sunday Mornings at the River,* and *The Wingword Poetry Prize.*

Through writing and teaching, Ambica hopes to remind others that while life may not come with a manual, it does come with poetry. And that is almost the same thing.

www.ingramcontent.com/pod-product-compliance
Lightning Source LLC
Chambersburg PA
CBHW042101150726
48005CB00033B/1495